D1268379

Olga's Dreams

fal

fal poetry

Keeping House	Bill Mycock
Dear Shadows	DM Thomas

Olga's Dreams

Victoria Field

fal

First edition 2004

ISBN 0-9544980-0-3

Cover design by Cassie Young

Cover image: *Russian Venus* by Boris Kustodiev by permission of the Nizhny Novgorod State Art Museum, Russia

Published by

Fal Publications
PO Box 74
Truro
TR1 1XS

www.falpublications.co.uk

Printed by

R. Booth Ltd
Antron Hill
Mabe, Cornwall

To Don, with love

Contents

Acknowledgements

Thanks are due to the editors of the following magazines and anthologies where some of these poems have previously appeared:

Magazines:
HQ Poetry Magazine, Le Voci della Luna, Poetry Cornwall, Poetry London, Poetry Wales, Raw Edge, Staple, The North

Anthologies:
Chatter of Choughs, ed Lucy Newlyn, Signal Books, 2001
Spirit of a King, ed Les Merton, Palores Press, 2001
Twenty Years of Twentieth Century Poetry, ed Donald Measham, Staple, 2001

Broadcast:
Radio Three *The Verb* commissioned *Register of Arrivals and Sailings No 22*

Web:
www.scriberazone.co.uk

Introduction

Do not sing to me again
Your songs of sad Georgia.
They bring to memory
Another life, a distant shore.

Alexander Pushkin 1828

The poems here do not mention Georgia, although it is a country I have visited several times and love. They do, though, attempt to bring to memory the many other lives that inform my present one by invoking the distant shores of earlier experience. Pushkin's poem addresses a 'beauty', asking her to desist from singing her sad songs and yet there is a strong sense that he is, in fact, enjoying them and the memories they evoke. Many of my own poems describe experiences of sadness and I have derived real satisfaction from working and reworking them into songs I would wish to sing again.

Writing poems became important to me when I first discovered the pleasure of enjambment and internal rhyme. I was eight years old, attempting to convey the excitement of Christmas in verse. I no longer have the poem but I remember how much I enjoyed the way the line about 'the girls and boys' flowed into the next one describing their 'joys, that would know no bounds' when they unpacked 'their sacks of toys'. That same Christmas, I was given *A Puffin Book of Verse* compiled by Eleanor Graham, first published in 1953 and full of traditional poems, sorted into such wholesome categories as 'In Holiday Mood' or 'Homely Things'. The poem that struck me most at that age was Kubla Khan and, even now, the phrase 'In Xanadu …' with its implication of reality mixed up with fantasy, gives me a unique thrill. Now that I have travelled, although not to Xanadu, I can recreate a similar sensation when I begin writing a poem with a specific place in mind, whether it's 'in Moscow' or 'in my grandmother's kitchen'.

I grew up in the country, in a scruffy part of Kent and was quite solitary, enjoying bike rides, woodland walks and endless hours curled up with a book. The old-fashioned girls' grammar school I attended was a bus journey away which mercifully excluded me from extra-curricular netball and the like, leaving more time for reading and daydreaming. The weeks were punctuated by Saturday visits to Ashford Library and, when I eventually moved from the children's section, where I had been becalmed for

years by Enid Blyton and fairy tales, up to the adult section, I decided to approach the huge quantities of books in a systematic way. This led to me being instantly hooked on philosophy, psychology and religion – all on the first shelves, next to the door, at the beginning of the Dewey Decimal categorisation. Had I entered the library by another route, I might well have become passionate about the history and geography of Antarctica instead. At home, I was reading Freud and Jung (through a glass darkly), and at school, during the long, laid-back sixth form years, I discovered Gabriel Garcia Lorca and Al Alvarez's *The New Poetry* – an overdue counterpoint to *A Puffin Book of Verse* and a different kind of thrill. Psychology and poetry, poetry and psychology became the twin obsessions that took me out of myself and, simultaneously, deeply into myself.

Then I got busy and distracted until in the past seven years, I have found ways of combining those twin early interests. I am fortunate to work using poetry with many different groups of people and am continually fascinated by its power to communicate subliminally as well as consciously. Thomas Ogden has described psychoanalysis as 'a conversation at the frontier of dreaming' and poetry, too, with its symbolic and metaphoric shorthand, has the power to speak to us as directly and mysteriously as dreams.

This collection contains those poems I am prepared to abandon, even if they will never be truly finished. I could not have completed it without the help of many gifted, generous teachers, including all those, most at a distance, who make space for poetry to be heard in an increasingly noisy world. In particular, I want to thank D.M. Thomas who gave me many kinds of permission and the late Peter Redgrove, whose poetic generosity and courage remain an inspiration. Thanks also to Bill Greenwell, who acted as midwife to several of the poems that appear here.

Victoria Field
Truro
August 2004

1

Another Life, A Distant Shore

The Wind Man

after Lorca

The pale sun turned her face
when the wind came to rape me
Cows crying for their calves
in the black Suffolk fields
fell silent as stars

I let his broad hands
push me high on my swing
He lifted my Sooty-and-Sweep
blue dirndl skirt
and whispered of oceans
and aeroplanes

The wind lived in my pillow
blew through my dreams
He followed when I pedalled
hard down to Folkestone
took the number 10 bus
met gypsies in Hastings

He lured me from the white towers
where the English live
We drove the magpie road
to Uzbekistan, took ponies
through the Amazon
fed white peacocks at Shangri-La

I tried to escape him, descended
the earth's dark centre
washed my wounds in red rivers
emerged, clear and clean as a lily
but he was there to reclaim me
flashing his sword in his fury

Bright angels vanished
as he moistened my lips
with gin and warm milk
quickened the waves on the sea
tied my ankles to the moon

My violator, my warm wind
taunts me
with gardens and marmalade
He makes me beg for it
for Saharas
Siberias.

Vague Memory

The church was classical
We held hands, it was warm

Tourists were elsewhere
The man was selling something

We bought whatever it was
because he was alone there

and he was old or maybe
it seemed cheap at the price

Then he wanted his photo taken
and he laughed at having no teeth

for the picture that just fell from the shoebox
of the day we bought something

from an old man outside a church
somewhere on an island, once.

Sergei Kuriokhin Wasn't My Lover

Last night I dreamt of Russia, rivers
and how ten years ago those fingers
didn't play my breasts, my sex or my skin

although I know how they longed to
Your show thrilled me with its loud and mocking mix
of rock and goats and marching bands – sheer noise aroused me, as did

the naked men who posed as statues around the walls
of Liverpool's St George's Hall
They winked at me so I took them home and had them all

I'd die if I didn't see you again – the next night
swopping leather for earnest beards, I watched you play jazz at the Bluecoat, but
spent the concert in your Petersburg flat

having you enter me time after time
forgetting the keys, you lifted my lid, plucking me senseless, making me scream
Your bow played all my inner selves

and you shouted as you ran up and down
my soft bones and
down and up. It was winter. Or summer

in any case, the window was blank and white
Anna Akhmatova couldn't sleep for the noise
she threw Modigliani's red roses

across to us lovers, and I trailed the petals
when I left, getting lost in the yards within yards
I was resting outside the Museum of Atheism

when four fluffy faced boys saw my jeans
and approached
Smoke On the Water? asked one

Yes I said. *Free love?* asked another
and I plunged my tongue into his mouth, tasting vodka and bitter tobacco
Ten years ago

more or less, more and less
I tell the woman who asks what I dream
She's in love with me, and

though she'd never say it, the sun goes in
when I leave at the end of an hour
I tell her, Sergei was just the first of thousands

of my Russian lovers, in cities where rivers flow one way
and poetry pulls in the other. I had them under the bells

of ancient churches and took them deep in their woods
among insect-loud birches
and once at the Bolshoi, I bribed the attendant well

made a nest from the furs then
loved through Giselle.
Anais Nin, another of my lovers

only lies when the truth needs improving.
I've never needed to. Radio Three dreams with me
tonight's *Impressions* will feature Sergei

(the soft chimes of your fingers on the keys)
Kuriokhin and his legacy to jazz.

Waiting, Siberia

A stuffed mammoth stands
in the Institute of State and Law

Patted, it rocks slightly, sticky pelt
sighing prehistoric dust

The windows are layered with grey
fossilising the distant fuzz

of new leaf on the birches. Scents of pine
retreat stoat-like

from the stale hall where a woman
with slippers spreading like fat seals

sluices old water
across the cracked floor

It is quiet. The mammoth mourns
A professor looms to greet me. His eyes

are huge stones, his voice soft
with moss

We shake hands in the Institute of State and Law
Somewhere else, it's spring.

After Akhmatova

Petersburg, 1998

Her small room still houses the card table
on which stands the ashtray
where she burned, ceremonially
the manuscripts of her poems

The tall trees in the overgrown garden
still sense the sad smoke that slid
over them from that white window
half a century ago

as does the old woman on the bench beneath
rhythmically shuffling
her slipper-clad feet
in dead leaves

as she mutters
the long-remembered verses
remembers
the long verse-filled years.

Storm, Moscow

Was it madness, I ask myself, to be taken in by
the way small clouds sped across the matt blue Moscow sky

and assuming rain was faraway, to wear that
flimsy dress and let the sun fall hard like paving, flat

against the skin of shoulders, arms and knees
so that I arrived brushing away blossoms fallen from the trees

onto my skin which longed for the touch of your fingers
that lay in your lap, broad-tipped and muscled, and lingered

over the programme you had bought already and picked up from my chair
when I came in hot from behind the dusty haze of city air

hanging over the river whose grey sinews reflected high small clouds
and the chair you pulled next to yours was so close I inhaled

the happy scent of onions on your breath and mine went in and out
too quickly and my fingers slid at random like tiny river trout

across my shoulders where the plane tree flowers had landed
when I left the car for the gallery where the band had

set up microphones and piano on a night when no one was expecting rain
and you showed me the programme in square Cyrillic and I feigned

understanding, all the time wanting to touch your springy hair
curled like the leaves were a month ago, all sweet and new in the rare

hope of summer coming down the Moscow river, counting bridges
as I counted the dates we'd had, the dancing, drinking, late-night raiding of the fridges

all without a single kiss or caress, no expectation of storms or thunder
and we settled back to hear the fat bassoon, piano, saxophone and I wondered

why there was sand on the gallery floor and clouds back-projected on the wall
behind the musicians, which somehow made me sad and happy and I cried for all

the brightness of the city falling from the summer air and then we drank
tiny shots of vodka and chatted to friends and thanked

the moon-faced man on the big bassoon and as we left the tiny yard
heaven gave way to rain and your sudden arm across my shoulder felt as hard

and heavy as a knotty branch of a lush plane tree and juicy rain drops touched my tongue
we laughed and I loved your arm in the mad way I love daisies as we began to run

to the car and drove over many Moscow bridges, my dress wet beneath me and all
the city's onion domes alive with gold, your head out of the window so the rain could fall

into those clouds of curls, then home to mouths on mouths as sweet as raspberries
and thighs soft as mushrooms growing under lightening-blackened trees

the loud surprise of rain and you, a world suddenly all in shades of blue?

Afghan Market

Peshawar, 1997

I run to avoid the sudden storm, cut
a pale path through the forest of brown eyes
enter a four storey *caravanserai,* rickety stairs
smells of rain on rubbish

The gold-sellers in the alleys outside are sleek
trading in guns and opium, *Allah* and America
but here a thousand shabby households
are piled high and going cheap

Tired faces on dusty carpets proffer me
sad smiles and Russian teapots, lapis on dulled silver
iftah bread and prayers, lewd winks, and all
the paraphernalia of Silk Route-treading horses –

things that once were somebody's things
from places where people once lived

In the rainy dusk, deep in the dirty inner city
I buy blue glass that shines like a tropical sea
and feel only the pity
the pity.

Purdah

We only want what's best for men
They are at risk, you know, from the prying
eyes, or worse, from women who can't be
trusted to control their lust

Confronted by the broad planks of a youthful chest
more than suggested by a well-cut shirt or
the round firmnesses of buttocks on a bicycle
their wanton fingers itch for relief

For their own freedom and safety, let's
get those manly limbs enshrouded
Black is best and watch those ankles
or even the sun might be tempted

and something there is in men's hair
that is scandalous; those black curly
question marks caressing the nape of
the neck are provocation

and pouting lips with perfect teeth
spell pure damnation. The stubbled jaw
and almond eyes; a road for the lascivious
tongue, leading straight to perdition

To save us all, let's keep men hidden
so women's lust can't rise unbidden.

Seduction, Lahore

Standing by the fruit salad, you start to stroke my fingers
while we talk about art and build bridges across the cultural canyons

You fill your wine glass to the brim with Baileys
as I savour the wide arc of your stomach beneath its *shalwar kammeez*

You admire my outfit, my skin and my smile
and your resemblance to Rushdie gives me a frisson of dangerousness

Your fingers tingle a tattoo along my forearm
and the others start to dance to the latest Nusrat Fateh Ali Khan

You tell me well-rehearsed stories of courtly love, Punjabi style
and I simper and laugh in all the right places, enjoying the bullshit

You acknowledge the post-modern irony of this prelude
yet you persist in the myth of falling in love with my feet

You are patient enough to spend hours adoring my ankles
and you talk of eternity worshipping, in turn, each one of my moles

You stir cultural confusion when my big toe, later, yields to your tongue
and I wonder where my verrucas fit in
in this land of peripheral loves.

Pomegranate Juice

Pakistan was as unexpected
as the iron-rich redness
of the glass I was given at breakfast –

a fruit basket of colour
sweet-scented by girls in bloom –

its red as tender as the blood
of a nation whose passion softly
spoken belies its broken heart –

as confusing as the men who
call me Sir as a token of
respect; appeasers for their sex

leaving bitter on my teeth the taste
of women shrouded in silence
and the passivity of the poor

I never knew that hard, dry
fruit, over-populated by pips
could yield such subtleties

that the sun-toughened skin
would open to such beguiling smiles
that I'd want to drink it daily.

Cross Cultural Conversation

How many children you have?
You married?
How old you?
Thirty four and a virgin! Nice!

Advent Sunday

Mersea, Essex

The fisherman is robed in rubber
fat blue fingers smell of petrol, nets

A chipped plate, bread and wine
are set before us in the wooden shed

Freezers hum and ice is rattled
over last night's catch

A little boy rosy from the winter sun
gazes at the world God offers him –

oysters shimmering like silver hosts
mussels bright as his beating heart

fish for a multitude
and the miracle of his mother

ice and warmth
in a wooden shed on the shore.

Estuary Haiku

Trees scratch the hard sky
with long skeletal fingers
hating the winter

A thousand plovers
blown out into the wide sky
fall like paper cranes

The cormorant slides
off the rock like a shadow
and darkens the waves

Grey grass grows gold in
the sunrise; sun treads shyly
sensing her power

Birds speckle the sky
like a dusting of spilt pepper
too small to be named

The mud reflecting cloud
can be very confusing
Is it earth or sky?

The slow tide rises
surprising the sleeping birds
Mud becomes water

Siberian geese
are happy; honking to us
This winter, this warmth!

On Martinique

for Bertha Mason

She came to me suddenly; a tidal wave
high as the palms, a cold wall
down which slid small fishes
mouths gulping strange air which gave

no succour. And there we were
in evening dress, fans, programmes
a twitter of Parisian conversation
when the volcano began to shudder

from some gut-deep pain, sending convulsions
through the archipelago of our cool hearts
Before it all collapsed, I had heeded nothing
but the butterflies in the forest of her hair –

they flew in a cloud of wing-beats as I bent
her backwards over the bed; mostly tiny
brown and orange, just a day's gift of life
but one, cobalt, giant, slow, emerged

wings beating a syncopated reply to my heart
echoing my blue eyes as they stared at the leafy
depths of her dark folds. It was the *morpho,*
the rare one, the colour of heaven, longed-for

redemption. Bertha, I glimpsed flying from your hair
purity; a blue that striped the scraps
of sky above the forest, cooling the heat of volcanoes,
diluting the blood-red *planteur* in my white hand

And, then, hot lava descended, warping trombones
and twisting church bells into witching sticks.
I saw the butterflies take flight
and the Caribbean turn black
and knew that fire
would always be where you are…

on the damp moors, in the dusty attics
in the way you screamed in terror at the grey
the endless grey.

Bardsey Island

On Bardsey Island, I build a bivvy
from my baby's bones
and let the white wind whisper to me
through its gap-toothed walls

My baby's ear is a shell
washed up onto the shore
telling me *hey diddle diddle* as the sea
chuckles the pebbles around my feet

On Bardsey Island, I gather the souls
of the good and the bad and the damned
and play them face-down like patience
to trick the world into making her whole

A fat red heart comes rolling towards me
surprised, like an adder in the bracken
and her smiles bounce through the clover
to the chink of spades in flinty graves

From Bardsey Island, to make it all come right
I set sail in a coracle to Cornwall
went spinning with the flying fish
then walked the dusty road alone to Rome

Countries popped up, colourful as picture books
My knees bled on the stairs to Roquemadour
but still, *fee fie fo fum,* my Bardsey baby is no more
The angels have won and taken her home.

2

Sex, Death and Eggs

Night Out With The Girls

i.m. Anne Sexton and Sylvia Plath

Sometimes, when the nights are soft and dense with darkness
you stand either side of my bed, whispering
offering to save me from weight
tempting me with death

You say, hey, he isn't heavy like a boulder
he's a ping-pong ball you can blow over
the coffee cups and laugh at
as pretty as pills, as light as gas

You invite me to Boston and we three
drink too many Martinis and invite him
to join us. He sits grinning
as innocent as his empty chair

You are better acquainted and older
than me and can tease him
He is nothing more than the handwriting
missing from the Christmas cards

He's the wobbling memory of a face
unseen for years, the utterly
inconsequential pet no longer
at the door. You smile and stroke my hair

You clever, clever angels
convince me he's a toy suitable for
women of loveliness
His nothingness moistens my lips

We drink and laugh and I leave
the bar with the blank-eyed boy
I take him home and call him mine
and stroke the long tunnel of his back

He's here, he's here beside me
He's sleeping.

Going Back

Today, I'll show you this ordinary street of semi-detacheds
strewn along a village hillside where my childhood years
drifted, each into the other, as I gazed long hours waiting
for the bells to end the long school days and saunter back to what
were then the brand-new houses of Prospect Way – owned by young
families whose lack of cash led to pampas grass planting and red paintwork
as imaginative changes to the standard boxes they'd saved so
hard for and where, outside, their children in the bouncy ways of those days
played on space hoppers, pogo sticks and bicycles in the tiny turning bay
until the slow decay of time crept across the street like fog and
sticky teenage nights drowned out our mums' favourite Jimmy Young with
T-Rex and worse – the years took on a sway of dramas and disasters
that tidy gardens couldn't keep at bay; the husband who worked away and did not
come home, the slow cancer deaths of one mum, one dad, the man who left his
wife for a boy, came back and stuck a hosepipe in the exhaust pipe of his car
and said goodbye that way – here's twenty seven, decades scruffier and several
owners later, the pampas grass my parents had begun now wild and tall.

The children have different faces but their games remain the same
and I hear, in spite of all those years, Jimmy Young still plays.

St Elizabeth's

The hospital smell
follows me into the bus

It sits on my hair
like a sad ghost

It smells like something
I must have lost

I count my fingers
carefully.

A Small Life

It wasn't without violence
this so-called going-to-sleep
this letting go of a world
of sunshine, tin openers and dawn prowls

Her eyes widened
to take in a high
winding road with its
hard-to-climb pines along the way

Her eyes widened
to become dark wells
where buckets swing
full of rotting leaves

Her spine narrowed
into spikes and the dense
fur suddenly thinned
as pointless as fluff over twigs

After the needle
I felt her life holding on tight
coiling itself around her heart
Then the poison kicked in with its vicious kick

and the life flew out of
her mouth in a rush
Her surprised tongue
followed it and flopped

A small life
just hung there, like heavy air
where once
her breath had been.

Unconscious Bus

The top deck has familiar faces
my sister as a baby
and one behind the other
twenty versions of my mother

Picasso, Christ, Clinton and Jon Snow
sit where you should, please
offer your seat when
male archetypes get on. Turning

at the top of the stairs
gives the pleasure of seeing
old friends from school or sometimes surprises
Why it's the Queen! or Princess Di

They'll tell you why they're there
Clinton for sex of course
the Queen likes a game of Scrabble
Christ settles for tea and a ciggie

Some stay on the bus for years
others for a stop or two
chatting among themselves
complaining about my life or the service

The lower deck is stranger
I don't know them so well
the Chinese soldier in his boat in the reeds
a woman whose face dissolves

the man in a balaclava lurking at the back
who might pull a knife
while pretending to read
about cheap fares to Eastbourne

The conductress dressed as a clown or nurse
says *Fares please* but they all disappear
so it's just coats sitting there
and forgotten shopping

The unconscious bus trundles on
past the man in the gutter and the beauty shop
where I see you waiting and press the bell
over and over, to get it to stop.

The Henhouse

When my father died
my mother made sounds
like a hen all night long.
I lay in my bed next door
listening to her crooning
as she washed him. I heard
an electric razor for the last time
in our house of women –
my own men later
preferring the slop and scrape
of lather, blade

The soft burble
of her henhouse voice
didn't stop
when she removed the snaky
catheter from the limp penis
that mocked him during
the long months of dying.
I was not then aware of the secret
nurse-knowledge of stopping
the anus with cotton wool but thought
he looked fine in his expensive
now oversized suit

The busyness of her chicken-
scratching, opening drawers
and tidying ties carried on
when she saw me and said
You need to go for the eggs
It was a school day but instead
of taking the bus to the town
I walked a mile along lanes
clutching a 50 pence piece
to the scruffy house of the man
who kept too many birds

The eggs were almost alive
and perfect, as eggs always are
They sat safe in the cardboard
caress of an egg box
I walked home, slow
as drizzle turned to weak sun
meeting halfway my grandmother
gnarled with grief, her arms
held wide open
like an old black hen
warming her wings after rain.

Woman in the Tub

after Degas

I felt that day like a flower
a lily blooming on a cast iron leaf
as if forests had found their way
into our crumbling Parisian rooms

Rose petals fell from my belly
trailing red between my secret thighs
I fell asleep a girl but that morning
dried a woman's form

the towel touching me as a lover would
my precious living ache warm
inside – a flower and a wound –
not just a woman in a tin tub

and her painter watching
the heavy circling of sun and moon.

Grandmother

Sea's freezing
smells of old weed and sewage
I'm always eight
hair rats' tails, stiff with sand and salt
wind whipping my legs

Granny combs without mercy
she's gigantic, a tank
carapaced in a black-boned costume
legs tree trunks planted white
creepered by blue ropes

Grandad silent behind a paper behind the windbreak
drinks sweet tea from a flask
tasting of old soup carefully
doesn't watch while she peels me
punishes my modesty with gritty towels

She died briskly couldn't complain
about slack hospital corners *et cetera*
this year's fruit rots in the garden
her jam jars accrue in the bottle bank
her voice in each soft smash –

It's a grand day for the beach.
Grandad will drive. It'll do us good.
Have you been? Wash your hands.
Eat your prunes.
It's not cold, once you're in.
It's not cold –
Once you're in.

Ash Wednesday

If I had an empty plate
and I held it out to you
asking for succour
with what would you fill it
this plate as round and pointless
as a barren belly?

And if I told you
my mouth was dry
from my days in the desert
would you fill my cup
with wine or air or kisses
or bless me with simple water?

If my hunger and thirst
can't be contained
on a plate, in a cup
how will you slake them
these needs that are
deeper than oceans?
How will you slake them?

Ophelia Goes Home in Middle Age

She was a fool to visit the scruffy village
from where the once-a-day bus
still trundles to nowhere

The school looked a dump
and the shop still sells
its special selection of stale and old

The boy she adored has turned fat
cold and grey. It's let-down and mizzle
in Memory Lane. The rosemary and violets

are obscured by the rain – only dog shit remains
along her old childhood track
Ophelia knows you should never go back.

Good Egg

It's a plum of an egg
in its shiny red wrapper
nestling – as the estate agents say
in an artful scatter
of pretty blue bricks

Around it, a savoy-cabbage swirl
of tossed green leaves
flavoured with caraway
by some clever cook
to keep her guests guessing

There are splashes of paint
yellow as sunshine
and flowers hidden in soft folds –
the whole palette wreathed
in primary smiles

It's a psychedelic summer of love
for this happy egg as it lies there
waiting for its unwrapping
its gift of chocolatey chins
smug in the knowledge
of just how good it is.

Bad Egg

I was once introduced
to 'the white sheep of his family'
How we laughed and he most of all
liberated by his relatives' bad deeds and weird ways

Now, I suspect I am an egg gone bad
wearing red and green in tones that don't go
not quite true like clothes from the Co-op
colours that look like they smell, stale and old

A bad egg appears suddenly like fungus
on a beech tree or a scatter of skin tags
on back and belly. It's your fingers sinking
into the slimy black last potato in the sack

My crinkled lips disown bad deeds
proving me worse than ever –
tell them you are a rotten egg and watch them retreat
It's no laughing matter.

Tides

The wind has scribed the sand
with unknown names in tongues
I'll never hear nor understand
Rivers, iron-dense and dark
link womb and sea, the hinterland

Love's failed again. What good
a passion spent? It cost so much
and still was insufficient

The turning tide will erase the day
No sea defence can keep the years at bay
There was nothing there
and nothing here again today –
just a cradle for the empty air
the space between my arms and hair.

The Secret Language of Women

On the net, I enter, unidentified
a world of women
having abbreviated sex –
TTC dominates their lives

No raunchy sex –
they coyly BD their DH's –
no one mentions a lover
They do it F2F and after

put a pillow under buttocks
Oral pleasures are reserved
for the 2WW when the baby dust
has passed – SOD for some men

is a bit of a sod
They are intimate with their cervixes
CP, CM, CF – the differences are subtle
and change with the days. The moon

is too poetic to mention
Did you EWCM this month? Did you see the
blessed egg-white in your panties?
There's no shame in this private space

It's a signal for SOD right now!
I called him at work, he came right over!
We BD'd all afternoon! O is ovulation
not orgasm, although one message thread

claims the latter might help
The 2WW is the worst, it's a killer
The women pray for each other
sprinkle virtual baby dust in the chatrooms

pair up as CBs – not pedalling
through leafy lanes but sitting
in late night rooms counting CDs –
their long repeating days

There's not a lot of LOLs
during the DPOs
Your BBT holds the key
The women share graphs

recommend special thermometers
£12 at Boots. Will it stay up
to nurture a possible bun in the oven
or crash when Aunt Flo announces her visit?

AF is a bitch (although that's not a word they use)
Just as they wonder
whether they've waited
long enough to take an HPT

just when they disappear
from the TTC page
to compare notes next door
on Early Pregnancy Signs

she arrives
But they never lose hope –
after shared tears on CD1
it's back to cutting the coffee, no fags –
its fish and loose pants for DH
and more F2FSOD.

Like them, I hesitate
to invite Aunt Flo in
but when she flings back the door
in her wild red dress

with her kick-ass, fuck-you attitude
takes me out in her fast car
far from the land of baby dust
for coffee, a drink and a smoke

for complicated sex and selfishness
to an earth-life, a work-life
where no babies
float by counting their toes –

she's all the company I want
Until, two weeks later
the gentle moon rises and
I wonder, did I O ?

Was that EWCM?
Can DH be persuaded
to make love F2F?

And I go, secretly,
late at night, unidentified
to meet them – the women
on the websites.

Key:

Aunt Flo	– menstrual period
BD	– bed dance ie sex
BBT	– basal body temperature which fluctuates during the menstrual cycle
HPT	– home pregnancy test
CB	– cycle buddy ie a woman on the same day of her cycle
CD	– cycle day
CF	– cervical fluid
CM	– cervical mucus
CP	– cervical position
DH	– darling husband
DPO	– days past ovulation ie when a woman might be pregnant
EWCM	– egg white cervical mucus indicating high fertitility
F2F	– face to face
HPT	– home pregnancy test
LOL	– laugh out loud
O	– ovulation
SOD	– sex on demand
TTC	– trying to conceive
2WW	– two week wait ie after ovulation before a pregnancy test can be taken

Forget-me-nots

A constellation of blue eyes
that cannot look this way

Insistent names, calling out
with nothing at all to say

A frilled and speckled counterpane
with no small soul asleep

A dancing, posing prettiness
but no lock of hair to keep

A scattering of loveliness
that won't take shape or grow

I'll remember you who never were
and can neither come nor go.

Drought

Yesterday she walked
a dry river bed
awash with spikenard

A hundred red
rose petals fell
through her belly

staining her petticoats
She took the gypsy's
satin sewing box and set

about the stitching
of her wounds made
wide by heat

But the wounds
couldn't be mended
The stains spread

like fig leaves
and the petals fell on the
stones and dust – there

where jewelled fish
once swam to a yellow moon.

Jumping

There is a moment when you are deep within me
and I am balanced on that exquisite pearl
when my world becomes boundless
my skin sounds like it sparkles
my breath is a thousand shades of blue

inside I grow like summer grass
my lips sail oceans
my heart wraps itself in the softest silk
my eyes smell like coffee and roses
thoughts scatter like sweet papers in the cinema

my back is an altar with candles
my thighs are struck by lightning
my breasts are continents
and my toes recite Shakespeare
on the top of Everest, backwards

and I ask you, *Shall I?*
and you answer, *Yes*
and the best of it is returning to earth
and your arms and your kissing away of my tears.

Some Reasons Why I Love You

from the video instruction manual

You are, for example, switched on
You are remote

You quickly and easily find my start button
You perform

You stand by, for example, my figure
Confirmation

You are desired
Every time

You decrease, for example, my search function
You let me find you.

Greek Salad in Northern Latitudes

The menu promised Mediterranean
heightened senses
an orgy of authenticity

Aroused I longed for the lusciousness of love
in the warm flesh wetness of
just-cut tomatoes

I wanted the salty surprise of the sudden juice
of olives as the stone
rolls round my teeth

and the brave constancy of cheese
agile with goat bells
fearless on the high crags

I wanted to bear the aliveness
of a bitter onion, rough-cut
like a lover's rejection

and the lemony sharpness
of rekindled wanting in the aromatic
caresses of a good fresh-pressed oil

Instead, a chemical tomato, a ration of passion
in the slack flesh of old olives
the cheese in its condom of extra-strong plastic
unfaithful to food

The air-conditioning deodorized my dream
of its singing scents of sun-singed thyme
and chilled its midnight seas
that were once as dark and warm as wine.

End of the Affair

I never told you I was wise,
I always knew I was a fool.
It shouldn't come as much surprise.

I never told you I was wise.
I'm not telling any lies –

I didn't know there was a rule.
I never told you I was wise.
I always knew. I was a fool.

Left Out to Dry

Don’t go there. Don’t even
think of going there.
Okay, I am up here alone
but pity is the last thing I want,
the last thing.

Just because you’re part of a pair
knotted together in a dark drawer
or slotted one inside the other
in some complicated kama sutra
thing doesn’t mean I want to be.

Okay, I’m up here alone
but there aren’t that many places
for a single sock to go
and feel okay about herself
if you know what I mean.

I mean, take parties. I mean
take your bloody parties. No one
wants a single sock at their party
You’re either sad or you can’t be trusted,
dangerous – a sock with her skirt too short
and too much lipstick.

Single socks spell trouble. That’s
what they think. Next thing you know,
their own precious sock is springing out of his shoe
on a Saturday going round with his spanner or hammer
or power drill offering to fix things.

Last thing I want is some dreary
married sock with his sad eyes and DIY
trying to impress me with his inadequate tool kit.
If I wanted some shelves doing
I’d get a man in.

No, I don't go to parties anymore –
can't stand the tedium of the endless talk
about how their sock drawer
doubled in value even before
they put in a drawer-divider.

And I feel a nitwit as a single sock
sitting alone in the cinema
amongst all the pairs of socks
holding hands or sharing
their buckets of popcorn.

And what could be grimmer
than the single sock in the pub
desperate, cross-legged in a corner
with her second white wine spritzer?
Sad, or what?

But don't feel sorry for me
I've had my share of socks in my time
and I've nothing against pairs of socks.
If it works for you fine. It's just not for me,
that 'we-two-in-our-shoes' thing, No way.

We single socks have to accept
limited horizons, our kind of places.
I can go unnoticed quite a while
left flat-damp after the final spin
of the machine.

Sometimes I've been left
in the drier, getting hotter and hotter
a pathetic single sock dancing around and around
in hope of a partner.

Never again.
At least up here I can see it all.
Vests and knickers come and go,
pairs of socks flutter side by side.

Poor things. Better the wind and rain
day and night than a dark drawer
and a sweaty shoe,
knowing that wherever he goes
so will you.

So don't even think of pitying me.
Don't go there.
Don't even think
of going there.

My Affair with the Bat

You seldom made eye contact so I stared
unobserved at your tragus, that fleshy spike
in your extra-large ears pulsing sonar and clicking
locating you as it dislocated me

I offered only fruit juice and nectar
thinking it sufficient and sweet
but you sank your teeth deep into my neck
drinking me as we danced

Even so, I couldn't sustain you
Aztec Lord of the Underworld, you needed
several hundred innocent insects each day
more bodies than mine

I thought I'd shed you, shaken you off
with your sticky-tongued friends
no more erratic swishing and swooping all night
and shitting in belfries by day

but your seed, sown in September
slept through the snows and then grew
on the stony remains of my heart
And all that summer you haunted me

I'd find you under the floorboards
hanging from the shower curtain
every crevice contained you

You, my unwanted familiar
you vampire, Bird of the Devil
even nested in the flower vase
where I went to put roses –
his roses – as yellow and pure as the sun.

End of Summer

after Lorca's Sonnet of the Sweet Complaint

It hurts to sit here in this pub
as if in a boat with no moorings
while you steer by the yellow

phosphorescence of your eyes
laugh at far horizons, steadied by
the polished oak of your forearms

I'm the forgotten beach towel
damp with yearning
an ear-ring lost in the sand
the sly bar-cat casing the greasy pans

Look at the sighing River Fal
and its five o'clock shadow of cloud
I'm blowing past in the first of lost leaves –
the calm swan, gliding over her frantic feet.

Dark Angel

On hearing that the chough is returning to Cornwall

She wears red tights and her lips are blood
Her legs are scaly and she has shiny black tits
Her voice destroys the floral sound of the song birds.
It is the caw of crow. She sits

on my face at night, comes running in with
the autumn spiders. Sometimes I scream
as traces of web sew up my eyelids. Her lizard tongue
whispers as she shrinks me under her wings nightlong.

I disappear myself to warmer places.
I am sticky with chough. My tears run clear
into the dirty cliff top puddles.
Yet he welcomes her to this long country

to silence the hedgerows. Her coarseness doesn't
stick in his craw. He drinks her red legs like
a vampire and savours the blackness
the shadow, the loneliness.

I'm running away. My heart held like a wren
beats in my hands. She wheels above me
claiming my skies, the cliffs and the moor
A lark sings my requiem and songs for the pure.

He Steps Back From The Painting

He climbed out of my depths
and my blue eyes dulled to flat

When we were so close
how could he not love only me?

When we were so close
his body tumbled whole into my frame

Now, at a distance
I bore him

Now, the gallery's full of blue eyes
enticing him.

To Icarus

I would like
to hold your
feet and feel
the air rush
through my hair
as you soar me
up and up
into
the empty blue

I would like
the empty
blue
to fold itself
like wings around
my body
making it weightless
and as long and
as light as you

I like to think
Icarus
you have
no fear
I like
to think, Icarus
I could be
like you
winging it, winging it.

Whispers

I spend hours in the garden
deadheading roses
planted by women long dead

My hands float away from me
to Cornwall, Bardsey, Avalon

She's gone west, I hear them say
I hear them say, *Let her rest*

His kingdom come –
I am no longer Queen

Like a bone
I need sinews to stiffen me

Like the wood
I cannot see the trees

I am a drum
well able to beat herself

a song
sung to the wrong tune

(one someone you used to know
used to hum)

Like the sun
I am somewhere else at night.

Spring

Overnight, like mushrooms
my jowls have softened
into those of my mother

The riverbeds of my eyelids
have deepened –
my grandmother returns my smile

and someone has been scribbling
faintly on my forehead –
words I am not yet ready to read
once, never, eternity.

Wasteland

for Vivienne Eliot

It worked well for this man,
to have a waste land to which
to send his unwanted woman

Her unspeakable biology
turned the pure Antarctic
of his bed's uncharted linen

to rampant rose gardens
flowering out of season –
damp with thorns and metal

He'd watched the tentative
shoots of her creativity
creep between the well-swept paving

of his calculated path
their roots daring
to touch black earth beneath careful stone

and then, from the clean machine
of his orderly body
he'd excise the unruly weeds.

More than wastelands
he created universes
of distance where time warped

and she couldn't know which way was up –
in which she'd hurtle
praying for gravity –

in which she finally imploded
in the infinite black hole
of a small locked room.

Summer Solstice

The dark night
sinks into inky sea –

there's only a scatter of faint stars
a fingernail of moon

The Lizard bulks
in front of us, breathing –

behind, the purveyors of buckets and spades
are shuttered and closed

On the fanciful stage-set
of Falmouth's fine hotels, everyone sleeps

Some shadowy figures
shift on a restaurant terrace

and a man high in a bright window
cleans his teeth, admires his profile

It's colder than we thought
when we decided to leave

the chatter and sausage grease
of a summer barbecue

We discard clothes and shoes
for this private night ritual

A couple distant on the beach
whisper into the wind like prayer

We joke about ratios
of surface area to volume

as the almost-Atlantic
draws away our warmth

We gasp in its embrace, waiting for life
to kick back in

me, buoyed like a beach ball
fat as a seal, easily floating

you, a quick tadpole
shimmering past

We touch briefly
before swimming our separate ways

Some centrifugal force
beyond the sky, the stars and the moon

doesn't want our union
in the black womb of this water –

it waves us apart
and keeps us solitary – half-beings

in our element, in the half-light
of the shortest night.

Blackbird

Its warning cry cuts through
the wet dusk, turns fog to glass

sets my heart racing
in a squawking of wings

as if I, too, could take flight
make my getaway from cats and cars

and those invisible strangers
loitering in my autumn head

armed with their sudden
sharpened thoughts of you.

3

Here, Now

Early

The whole house is soft with sleep –
deep beneath waves of feathers

the people sink into slumber
The dog twitches, stretching

across the sofa and the cat curls
around her hidden head under the radiator

I spread gorse-coloured butter
over toast which crumbles like darkness –

my body slow with tenderness
for these dormant creatures, who

though touched by morning light, birdsong
wind, the faint roar of a waking world

stay far away, here but there, vaguely aware
of love, like breath, invading their dreams.

Along the A39 after the Jubilee

for Peter Redgrove and Penny Shuttle

We drive through
the cathedral of trees.
The oaks knobbly

with the calluses
of cathedral builders
are long to arch over us

The beeches sing
in the lacy voices
of boys to the

Kings and Queens
processing
in their cars

My passengers
become an owl
and a snake –

one's wise eyebrows
lifted to the living Lord
the other, lithe with love

and secrets. My engine
anoints itself
with Duckhams

its pistons
as precise as parades
The tyres roll on

like old rock stars
my carriage good
for many a year yet

I'm a Chicken Shed child
wanting to wave
my surprised hands

at the majesty of all of it –
this cathedral of trees

this road, a carnival of cars
dancing along in the sun.

Making Love To Jesse James By His Wife

When he unbuttons my dress
his nubbled finger fumbles
private against my breasts

When his eyes meet mine
he blinks as if the sweetness
is too much, too coarse, too fine

I run my tongue over the teeth
rubbed clean by his fingers
and linger on royal gold

Around us, an abandonment
of red wool, superfluous suits and colourful cravats
Words fit for ladies float on the air

and when we lie down
time stands still and his crooked foot
speaks of storms and torrents

I kiss the stigmata of his chest and thigh
then lose myself in the getaway
universe of him

A single star shines bright
in the deep, strange night.

Shadows

You can't remember who took that early photograph

Your face, at four, is, I'm absolutely sure
smiling at your mother as she crouches behind her Kodak
Every crease in your squashy cheeks and scrunched-up nose
deepens with a desire to smile her yours

Look how coyly you have raised your shoulder
turning sideways as you must have seen your sister do
so many times, posing just this side of provocative
when her father's camera weighed her, wanting

You are pure flirtation and delight, laughter
creating a halo of happiness around you
only too eager to *Smile!* for mummy
little arms stiff with the pleasure of pleasing

unlike your sister, sitting apart, flat, flat-on
knowing that she faces the competition
and loses. Your father, quizzical, proprietorial
smiles a half-smile, accepting his exclusion

Unaware of the drama of this criss-crossed love
and the cold and shadowed nights of future times
you, little one, are pure radiance, ignited by her gaze
The sun doesn't need to be told how to shine.

Along the River Fal

The wooden boat tethered to the tree
lifts as wider waters swell its under-
sand-held belly. It rises up as if to see
where the gaping river's heart will wander

Faraway, out to sea, the whales deeper, deeper go
where all is blue and dark and full of voice
They take that blueness, darkness and blow
it into empty air. And the tilting seagull makes its choice –

the wide ocean or this little creek where serenity
rests in stiller waters. It touches down
where a tethered boat may be
tugging at or against an ebb or flow –

deeper, higher, waking, sleeping – no one knows
where the hearts of whales and birds and boats will go.

Romance of the Moon

after Lorca

The moon above Maenporth
wears gold and bronze dresses

I look at her and look at her
Over her shoulder

comes the wild smile
of the Man-in-the-Moon

He holds her, his Moon-Madame
waist-wise from behind, firmly

I know him as the old poet
the man I gave my dreams to

the man whose lines lie
in a deep sea-place

The timid ones tell me to run
from the strange caves

the slippery rocks
this greedy moon and her man

who dress me in water-sequins,
have me dance to their tune

my feet and hands
as busy as boats

When the silver fish slides up beside me
alive with temptations

speaking of China
and oysters and oceans

the timid ones quiver –
but distantly, faint as far stars –

as I give myself up
and away from the land

to the sea, to the gold, to the air
to the Queen of the Moons and her man.

Aquilegia Vulgaris

He throws up his hands
at the Granny's Bonnets
growing everywhere
in our unlaced garden

Promiscuous
is what they are
he says and laughs –

he with his secret partners
he with his frequent trips
to Lanzarote
where only cacti
penetrate the harsh black earth

The Columbines flicker
in the breeze
shaking more seeds
into soft Cornish soil

They cop off with no one
but the garden they call home –
they are as faithful
as my grandmother
busy in her kitchen

producing tray after tray
of currant buns
from her ample ovens.

Chough

When I saw you in Wales where I walked
with the dark haired boy whose love I craved

you tipped in the wind like a kite. Stalks
of dandelions twisted and craned

as we did, thrilled at the sight of your
rare black form as it questioned the sky

the hills, the grass, asking why and what for –
you were there above and we below – our eyes

wings, arms and lips, feathers, beaks, skin –
the sums of our parts on these hills, in this world –

your racing above to where might be heaven
our feet on this earth, eyes looking at you?

We were naming you whole, making blackness be chough –
wanting to say it, as if plain words could be answers enough.

Custoribus et cato

In the days before electricity and street lights, the medieval clock in Exeter Cathedral depended on a cat to keep mice, rats and pigeons from chewing the ropes. Records show that a penny a week was paid to the 'custoribus et cato'; the vergers and cat.

Forget the vergers –

It was I, with my arching back
who carried the heavens across the sky

It was I, with the casual grace of my paw
set the moon rolling like a ball of wool

It was I, with the metal of my green gold eyes
spun the moon into fullness, month after month

My needle teeth sewed your time
as intricate as a bishop's cope

with pearls of days and golden threads of night –
fishermen and farmers, merchants and maidens

came to gaze at what I'd made. In the moonlight
my voice stretched to your glory on the rooftops

Now, I repent for the rats, take, eat the brown host
of a dirty penny, take, drink the milk of a virgin mother

then slip through the small door's smaller hole
from this tired, turning world, to the eternal other.

The Heart's Orchard

i.m. Cornish apples

Ben's Red my mother said, 'But flushed and streaked
with russet dots enough to give your tongue the hots.'

I preferred my *Blackamoor Red* who came to bed in acid green
a sweetie, he flushed dull purple when I told him I had been

up along the Tamar with *Colloggett Pippin* who plied me
with a cidery champagne and promised dumplings for my pain.

His tree was large but how could I resist the *Duke of Cornwall*
when he told me, though not a looker, he could be a real cooker?

and then came *Hockings Green*, a lover of warm wet weather.
'I'm good for cakes – and tarts,' he said 'I'm a wholesome fellow.'

Early Bower was pale and rather yellow and came a bit too soon.
Cornish Pine had tender flesh but suffered cankers on new moon.

My father said, '*Snell's Glass Apple* is easily maintained. Or how about
Venus Pippin – she's soft and juicy if you're otherwise entertained?'

My sister had *Sweet Merlin* and *Mannacan Primrose* on the side.
Pleasant, sharp and crunchy, sweet, they kept her satisfied.

To Wadebridge with *Tregonna King* until his branches began to sag.
I put him aside for Christmas and popped a *Pig Nose* in my bag.

But now those days are over, my lovers all long gone. Smoother types
with blemish-free skins from New Zealand, South Africa and France

try to woo me in their plastic coats and turn up in tasteless tarts.
'Get lost,' I say, 'Please go away. My heart is not for scrumping.'

It lies broken, gently rotting where the rabbits used to dance
among the daisies beneath the trees in the orchards of my past.

Register of Arrivals and Sailings No 22

Held in the library of the National Maritime Museum, Falmouth

GC Fox and Co
of Falmouth
have no truck
with the vagueness of waves

in copperplate hand
straight columns
they bring me the listings
of capable captains

Captain Brock
and a cargo of coffee
Captain Klocker
carrying coals to Corfu

Doubleday and Jones
with hides and horns and bones
ballast, salt
and cedarwood

scents of San Francisco
Trinidad and Zanzibar
Cienfuego, Alexandria
Salina, Old Calabar

Captains Carrigal and Kirby
potatoes from St Malo
maize and manganese
eight hundred tons of guano

their vessels sway like women
Catherine, Lizette, Germania
Madre, Madre Rosa
Olive, Matilda, Nina

others brag their conquests
Dominion, Star, Excelsior
Viking, Adolf, Edgar
Jupiter, Dictator

from Adelaide and Rangoon
Odessa and Bilbao
Milk River, Varna, Danzig
Guadeloupe and Aracaya

carrying nitrate, nuts and linseed
currants, wheat and rice
oil, ebony and boxwood
pine kernels from Grand Bassam

they come with leaking topsides
torn sails and stress of weather
men overboard, cracked pipes
shifting cargoes, lost propellers

Captains Cameron and Burns
Captain Storm and Captain Grey
Montevideo, New York, Cardiff
Tarragona, timber, coal

… my pumps are choked with listings
I collide with unknown barques
…images float
like boats …

but GC Fox and Co
of Falmouth
have no truck
with the vagueness of waves

they set it all down
in copperplate hand
in columns as straight
as those captains who came.

Petition

In Cornwall, the saints are sleeping
under billowing dunes. Sand blew in
and blanketed the churches
silenced the oratories and stilled the bell

These are saints without armies
drifting in on leaves or shells or stones
their voices soft and strong and long as wind
hearts smooth and white as bone

There's no Augustinian turning from the world –
no need when world is a muddy path
with primroses, squat trees, deep creeks
clefts in the cliffs and running surf

Here, bracken censes the holy wells
and pilgrims bring their private fears
Torn rags hanging from the twigs
are damp with moss and prayers and tears

Winds get ready to blow away the sand
and toll the bell for the limbless child
The saints will rise and arm themselves
with gentleness, seek out the wells

surprised to see, shimmering in dark water
their half-forgotten face again
and there, among the heavy fronds
miracles trickling with the rain.

Zennor

St Sennara trapped
the mermaid
in his small, grey church

She's now as silent
as the hard wood
of the old, dark pew

eternally looking
in her mirror for gulls
for boats, for pink, for blue

longing for her own hair
as it once was
at one with the waves.

Temenos

It's a small world I want now
just an oval lawn and hollyhocks
no horizons beyond the well-swept floor
the garden wall and the blue front door

A sacred space for the rituals of
writing, the welcoming of friends
prayerfulness and playfulness and
a curled-up cat where the sun comes in

warmth of a kitchen, simple wine
the eucharist of wet grass beneath
my morning feet and all creation
in the sudden bloom of a single lily

The earth can turn, wars begin
and Romes burn but leave me here
in these kind rooms
and let the priests and angels come.

Words

after Anne Sexton

Some words fly to Ararat
soft, white and singular

Others emerge from the conjuror's cape
I'm fearful of him and his wands and witchery

My words are quiet as toes in a shoe
and hidden like the nothing worn beneath a summer dress

My words want to fill your wellingtons with the thrill
of waves from the oceans

but they are unsteady, born too soon
and knot in my fingers like failed knitting

The poet said *Be careful of words*
I know – they trap my blood

to make black poppies on snow –
they love me, they love me not.

Invocation

Keep me from seeking simply
the light. Keep me from staying
too much awake. Take me into
the dreamtime, the half-light, the dim
and the dusk where moons and stars
might emerge, unfold themselves
slowly
like mysteries

Or might not

Keep me from certainties.

Biographical Note

Victoria Field was born in London in 1963. She grew up mostly in Kent, studied psychology at the University of Sussex and subsequently lectured in that subject at West Cheshire College.

She later joined the British Council and worked in cultural and educational affairs in Istanbul, Moscow and Pakistan and travelled widely and adventurously. She has an MA in Cultural Policy from the University of Warwick.

She now lives in Cornwall, an almost-island on the edge of Europe, where the wild landscape and the rich culture combine to create a uniquely inspiring environment. She works as a Poetry Therapist, combining her interest in psychology with her love of literature.

For further details, please visit www.falpublications.co.uk.